COLLEGE LIBRARY

**Please return this book by the date stamped below
- if recalled, the loan is reduced to 10 days**

Fines are payable for late return

Also by Bel Mooney

I don't want to!
I can't find it!
It's not fair!
But you promised!
Why not?
I'm scared!
Why me?
I wish!
I'm bored!

for older readers

The Voices of Silence
Joining the Rainbow
The Stove Haunting
A Flower of Jet

Bel Mooney

I KNOW!

Illustrated by Margaret Chamberlain

mammoth

First published in Great Britain 1991
by Methuen Children's Books Ltd
Published 1992 by Mammoth
an imprint of Egmont Children's Books Limited
239 Kensington High Street, London W8 6SA

Reprinted 1993 (three times), 1994, 1995 (twice),
1996 (five times), 1997, 1998, 1999 (twice)

Text copyright © 1991 Bel Mooney
Illustrations copyright © 1991 Margaret Chamberlain

The moral rights of the author and
illustrator have been asserted.

ISBN 0 7497 1134 5

A CIP catalogue record for this title
is available from the British Library

Printed and bound in Great Britain
by Cox & Wyman Ltd, Reading, Berkshire

Contents

I Know How To Do It!   7

I Know It's Mine!   14

I Know She Doesn't Like Me!   22

I Know You've Remembered!   33

I Know She's Awful . . .   42

I Know I'm Right!   50

I Know You Know!   57

I Know How To Do It!

For weeks Kitty had been saving her pocket
money, until her piggy bank was very heavy.
And one day Uncle Joe dropped in to see them
and gave her a whole pound! So at last she
could afford the special thing she wanted – and
came home proudly from a shopping trip with
her parcel.

'What's that, Kit?' asked Daniel.

'It's a kit,' said Kitty.

'No – *you're* a kit, so what's that?' he teased.

'It's something I'm going to make, all by
myself,' said Kitty proudly, taking the box
from its paper bag.

It was a model-making kit – the kind of
thing Daniel loved. 'A galleon, see?' said
Kitty, showing her brother the picture on the
lid.

'Great! Can I help?' Dan reached for the kit,
but Kitty snatched it away.

Just then Dad came in. 'What's that?' he asked.

'It's Kit's silly kit,' said Dan, sulkily, 'only I think she's too young to make it by herself.'

'I'm not!' shouted Kitty.

'You are, too!'

Dad took the box and turned it over in his hands. 'I used to love making things like this,' he said. 'Maybe you'll let me help you a bit, Kit-kat.'

'No,' Kitty said, tossing her head. 'I know I can do it all by myself.'

She went upstairs to her room and tipped all the parts of the model out on her table. One or two fell on the floor, but she didn't notice. In fact she was in such a hurry to get started, she could hardly bear to unfold the sheet of instructions. They looked so long and complicated . . . Kitty *knew* it must be easy to work out what to do as you went along.

She picked up two of the pieces and slotted them together. 'Of course,' she muttered to herself. 'They make the bottom of the boat . . . what's it called? . . . the hull! This is going to be easy.' And she reached for the glue.

About half an hour later, Daniel stepped into her room. 'How's the kit going, Kit?' he asked in a cheerful voice.

Kitty looked hot and bothered, but said nothing.

'Having problems?'

'No!'

Not long after that, Dad popped his head around the door and whispered, 'Can I come in, love?'

'No!' said Kitty. By now she was looking *very* hot and *very* bothered. There was glue in her hair, and one of the transfers for the sails was stuck to her cheek. By now the instruction leaflet was spread out and covered with grubby, gluey fingerprints, and small bits of galleon lay scattered all around.

'Are you all right, pet? Because I could easily help . . .' smiled Dad.

'No!' Kitty yelled. 'I *know* how to do it, so there!'

Dad shrugged, and disappeared.

Kitty struggled on. All the little fiddly pieces stuck together, then stuck to her hands. As the galleon got bigger it began to look rather odd. In fact, you would have to be *told* what kind of boat it was. But still Kitty went on. She couldn't ask for help, not now.

Mum and Dad were making supper together when at last – much, much later – Kitty rushed into the kitchen. 'Come and see my boat,' she shouted.

'Boat?' asked Mum. 'I thought it was a galleon.'

'Ah, just wait and see!' smiled Kitty.

Dad and Mum followed her into the sitting room where Dan was standing by the small table, laughing.

'It's not a galleon,' he spluttered, 'it's a wreck!'

Dad hid a grin. Mum looked anxiously at Kitty, expecting her to shout and scream. But instead she said, 'That's right.'

It was a strange but interesting sight. On an old piece of board lay the galleon, on its side.

One of the masts was hanging off, the other was broken. Bits of rigging lay scattered around, and the little paper flags drooped sadly. Kitty had painted the board sandy yellow, and stuck bits of wood and shells higgledy-piggledy all over it, so that it looked like . . .

'The sea floor!' cried Dad, suddenly understanding.

'Ooh, just look at the skeleton,' whispered Mum. Once, at Hallowe'en, Kitty had been given a pair of plastic skeleton joke earrings, and now one of them was lying near the boat, a few tiny circles of paper near its outstretched fingers.

'Pieces of eight, you see?' Kitty explained.

'Well dear,' said Mum, 'I must say I think you've been very imaginative to do all this.'

'Yes,' said Dad, 'it reminds me of all the stories about shipwrecks I used to read.'

Kitty looked rather superior. 'Yes, well, I told you I knew how to make the kit. But then I thought it was just a bit too easy, so I'd turn it into something more . . . er . . . interesting. Like this.'

And Daniel was the only one who didn't believe her.

I Know It's Mine!

Mum was in a good mood, for some reason, and Kitty always tried to take advantage of that! It was a beautiful sunny day, and as they passed the toy shop, Kitty pointed to the display of water guns in the window. These were big, black and fierce-looking – much better than ordinary water pistols.

'Look, Mum,' said Kitty, 'if I had one of those, Daniel and I could put on our swimming things and cool off in the garden, and you wouldn't have to take us to the pool. Oh please . . . !'

And, to her amazement, Mum said yes.

So now Kitty owned a splendid water gun, and couldn't wait to go next door and show William. She put on her bathing costume, filled the gun with water, and ran through the gap in the fence. She planned to call his name by the kitchen door, wait until he came out,

14

then give him a good soaking. She grinned to think of his wet clothes . . .

'William!' she yelled.

'Just coming,' came his voice from inside.

Kitty waited. Suddenly William dashed out, wearing his swimming trunks, and spraying water all around. Kitty squealed as she was showered, then her jet of water hit him full in the face.

Then they stopped and looked at each other in amazement.

They had the same water gun.

'Oh, this is going to be fun,' grinned Kitty.

'Hands up, or I fire!' yelled William.

Soon they were chasing each other all over the garden, and keeping both families at bay – because *they* were afraid of getting wet. Once or twice they put down their guns and had a rest, and then William took both to be refilled at his kitchen tap . . . Then the games would start again, in the hot sunlight.

Then something began to go wrong with one of the guns. It wasn't broken, exactly, it just didn't fire such a good, strong jet as the other one. Kitty squeezed and squeezed, but that seemed to make it worse, whilst the jet from

William's gun almost knocked her off her feet. He roared with laughter.

Kitty didn't like it.

'Give me *that* gun,' she ordered.

'Why should I?'

'Because it's mine,' she said.

'No, it's not – besides, how can you tell?' William held up the gun. Both were identical, of course.

'I just *know* it's mine,' said Kitty. 'You picked it up by mistake.'

'No, I didn't!'

'Yes, you did!'

They were quarrelling so loudly William's big sister Sally came out to see what was the matter. She shook her head. 'Really, Kitty,' she said, 'I don't see how you can say this one's yours.'

'You're just on his side 'cos you're his sister.'

Then Daniel came and joined them, and said exactly the same thing as Sally.

'Well, I think you should be on my side 'cos you're my brother,' sniffed Kitty.

Sally shrugged. 'Well, William, why don't you let Kitty have a go with your gun,' she said.

'Why should I?' he said crossly.

'Anyway, I know it's MY gun,' shouted Kitty.

Then, hearing the noise, both mums came out and asked what was going on. The children explained.

'I wish I'd never bought the wretched thing,' said Kitty's mum.

'So do I,' said William's mum, and sighed.

Then Kitty's mum held out both hands. 'Give me the guns,' she commanded.

The children obeyed, and she hid both guns behind her back. She seemed to be trying to swap them over, but that might have been a trick. 'Now,' she said, 'Daniel and Sally choose one, and say if you can *see* any difference.'

The two older children did as she asked, and inspected the guns. Of course, they could not tell them apart.

Now everybody looked at Kitty. 'Kit – are you sure you know which is yours?' asked Mum.

Kitty nodded – a bit slowly. 'All right then, show us,' said Daniel.

By now Kitty was confused, but wouldn't show it. She reached out and took the gun Sally was holding.

'All right, now fire it,' said William, standing beside her with the other gun.

But when they squeezed the triggers, the gun Kitty was holding sent out a really feeble spray, half the length of William's.

Suddenly she felt silly and wanted to cry.

'There – you see?' said her brother.

'But I don't think this one's mine,' she said, really quietly.

Then William surprised everyone. 'No,' he said in a very grown-up voice, 'it probably isn't. But you don't know for sure, and nor do

I. So I've got an idea, Kitty.'

'What's that?' she sniffed.

'You have that gun for today, and tomorrow we'll swap. We'll say neither is yours, or mine!'

Kitty smiled through her tears, and everyone looked relieved.

'I'll tell you one thing I *do* know,' she said.

'What's that?'

'I know you're my nicest friend,' said Kitty.

I Know She Doesn't Like Me!

One Monday morning Kitty went into the classroom to find someone sitting in her place, next to her friend Rosie. Kitty didn't like that one bit.

When Mrs Smith saw her stop and frown, she swooped over and explained in a loud voice, so all the children could hear, 'We've got a new girl with us today, Kitty, and we've all got to make Anita welcome. I've put her next to Rosie who's going to look after her, and you can go and sit next to Tom.'

Kitty didn't like Tom very much. He was the tall boy with red hair who used to call her Shrimp. Crossly she went to her desk to move her things. 'I've already done it for you, Kit,' said Rosie. 'Er . . . this is Anita Attra.' And she smiled at the new girl.

Kitty felt very jealous. What made it worse was that Anita was so pretty. She had very long

black hair in a single plait, and wore a long pink tunic over tight purple trousers.

'I'm pleased to meet you, Kitty,' she said in a small, shy voice.

'Me too,' said Kitty, and turned away to go and sit next to Tom.

'Hello, Shrimp,' he whispered.

Kitty jabbed him in the ribs. 'You said you wouldn't call me that any more, *Carrots*,' she hissed.

It was not a good start to the day.

At playtime, Kitty went across to Rosie, determined to get her friend back. 'Hey, Rosie, I've got some chocolate biscuits, and brought some stickers to swap,' she said.

'Sorry, Kit, but I've been told to show Anita all over the school,' said Rosie. 'Why don't you come with us?'

'No thanks,' said Kitty, turning away.

She played with William and some other children, and did the same at lunch time. At the end of the afternoon, she rushed out of school without even saying goodbye. She was quiet all the way home, until Mum asked what was the matter.

'Rosie's got a new friend, a new girl,' she said. 'And she doesn't like me.'

'Oh come on, what makes you say that?' asked Mum.

'I just KNOW,' said Kitty, and went to watch TV.

All week it was the same. Rosie stayed with Anita, and it looked as if they were becoming good friends. Anita was still shy, but Kitty thought she was being unfriendly.

Still, by Friday she was so sad because of

Rosie, she decided she just had to make an effort to like the new girl, if Rosie really liked her so much.

So, seeing Anita on her own for a few minutes, she marched up to her. 'Um . . . er . . . um . . . I just wondered if you'd like to

come to my house after school on Monday,'
she said.

Anita looked surprised.

'Oh but . . . I can't. I'm sorry, Kitty.'

'Oh, suit yourself,' said Kitty, and walked
away – just as Rosie came back.

'What was that all about?' Rosie asked
Anita.

Anita told her what had happened. 'She
didn't give me a chance to explain,' she sighed.
'It's no good, Rosie, I know she doesn't like
me.'

And at that very moment, Kitty was
standing in the cloakroom talking to William.
'I try to be friendly, but she's just stuck up. I
know she doesn't like me, and that's all there is
to it.'

'Well, if you look as cross as that . . .'
muttered William. Then, secretly, he went off
to have a word with Rosie . . .

On Saturday morning the telephone rang,
and it was for Kitty. She was really surprised
to hear Anita Attra on the line. 'Hello, Kitty,'
she said shyly. 'I just wondered if your mum
would let you come to tea with me on Monday
night?'

'But . . .' Kitty began.

'You see, it's a special day,' said Anita
mysteriously.

Kitty couldn't wait for Monday. From time to time Anita and Rosie would smile at her, but still Kitty didn't feel sure about them.

'Maybe she's only invited me to be polite,' she thought. 'But she doesn't like me really, I'm sure.'

She whispered to Rosie that she was going to Anita's house, expecting her to be surprised. But Rosie just looked knowing, and said, 'Me too.'

Mrs Attra was waiting by the school gate, looking beautiful in a scarlet sari. She had sparkling brown eyes, and shook Rosie and Kitty warmly by the hand. 'I am very glad to meet Anita's new friends,' she smiled. That made Kitty feel awkward.

When they got to Anita's house, Kitty couldn't believe her eyes. Although it was only October the house was decorated as if it were Christmas, with tinsel everywhere, candles, and twinkling fairy lights. It was so exciting.

'But what . . . ?' she gasped.

'I know what it is,' said Rosie, 'it's Diwali.'

'What's that?' asked Kitty.

Anita looked rather proud as she explained. 'It's a bit like your Christmas, Kitty – only in our religion. We're Hindus – you know? Anyway, we have this great celebration every October, and that's why I couldn't come to

28

your house tonight. So I thought I'd ask you here.' Then she looked shy again. 'I hope you don't mind?'

'*Mind?*' Kitty said. 'Of course I don't. But I thought . . .'

Just then Anita's mum passed them a plate of sandwiches and told them Mr Attra would be lighting fireworks in the back garden very soon.

'I know what you thought,' said Rosie.

Now Kitty felt embarrassed. 'Shut up Rosie,' she said. 'Hey Anita, why do you have fireworks?'

But Rosie wouldn't let her change the subject. 'My mum says all things are better out in the open – so, go on, Kitty, explain to Anita.'

'All right – er, I thought you didn't like me, Anita,' Kitty mumbled.

'But I *knew* you didn't like me,' Anita whispered.

'And that just shows how daft you both are,' said Rosie. 'You didn't give Anita a chance, Kit, because she was in your desk and everything. And Anita, because you decided she didn't like you, you couldn't be friendly to her. So it was just a silly mix-up.'

'That's right,' grinned Kitty.

'Time for food and fireworks,' said Anita happily.

They had a great time. The fireworks sent showers of bright sparks into the sky, whilst

Kitty and Rosie munched hot dogs and samosas with Anita and her three brothers. After the fireworks the Attra family all gave presents to each other, but they hadn't forgotten to wrap something for their visitors. Rosie and Kitty got a new purse each, which pleased them very much.

At last the doorbell rang, and Kitty's mother was there to collect them. As they thanked Mr and Mrs Attra, and said good night to Anita, Kitty suddenly felt a bit shy again.

'That was really lovely, Anita,' she said, 'and for once I was glad I was wrong.'

Anita grinned broadly. 'Will you play with me tomorrow?' was all she said.

I Know You've Remembered!

One Easter, just for a change, Kitty's family rented a tiny cottage in the middle of a wild moor. 'We'll probably stay at home this summer,' said Dad, 'but a spring holiday makes a nice change.'

At first, Kitty wasn't sure. It was rather chilly, and rained a lot, and sometimes she felt she would rather be at home with all her toys.

But they went for long walks, saw strange birds, and collected wild flowers – and she decided it was good to be away from the town. So perhaps this would be the best Easter ever.

Now Easter was always quite a special event in their family. They had certain traditions. Late on Saturday night Mum and Dad would go outside and choose a pretty branch for the centre of the table. They would put this in a vase, and then decorate it with pretty little painted wooden birds and eggs and rabbits. Mum called it their 'Easter Tree'.

On Easter Sunday morning the children go downstairs and find the 'tree' in the middle of the table, surrounded by chocolate eggs for every member of the family, and usually little presents wrapped in yellow tissue paper. Then Mum would draw funny faces on their boiled eggs with Kitty's felt-tips.

The children always acted as if the Easter table was a surprise – although, of course, it was the same every year. The funny thing was, it always *felt* new and exciting.

But this year they weren't at home, so Kitty was afraid it wouldn't be the same. But she had seen Mum putting the box with all the Easter ornaments into the car, and a huge bag she knew contained the chocolate eggs. Mum warned her the cottage was a long way from any shops, so Kitty bought three cream eggs before they left home.

On Easter Sunday morning Daniel and Kitty woke early, and heard Mum moving about downstairs. 'I hope it's all the same,' she whispered to her brother.

'It will be – knowing Mum,' said Dan.

'Ooh, I love Easter,' said Kitty – and Dan agreed.

At last they heard Mum shout, 'OK, kids, you can come down,' and they clattered down the stairs to the kitchen. The table looked as pretty as ever, and seemed crammed with goodies. Mum had already painted faces on the boiled eggs, and stood by the stove, smiling.

Dad came into the kitchen behind the children, yawning.

'Sit down, everyone,' said Mum, 'before the eggs go hard and cold.'

At Dad's place, and at Daniel's, and at Kitty's was a painted boiled egg, a large chocolate Easter egg, and a little presesnt wrapped in yellow tissue.

But at Mum's place there was a plain boiled egg – and nothing else.

At first Kitty didn't notice – then she rushed upstairs to get her cream eggs, giving one to each of the others. Daniel did the same with three chocolate rabbits he had brought.

Then Kitty smiled across at Dad. 'Now you can go and get what you've brought for Mum,' she said.

But Dad had a strange look on his face. 'Oh dear,' was all he said.

'Go on, Dad – don't tease!' said Daniel.

Dad just shook his head and looked a bit worried.

'Oh, I know you've remembered,' said Kitty, 'so I'm going upstairs to get it from your room!'

And she ran upstairs to search their bedroom. But she found no grand chocolate egg in a fancy box, nor any little gift wrapped in tissue paper. Kitty simply couldn't believe it. She walked slowly downstairs and stood in the doorway.

'Dad – I *know* you remembered?' she said, in a questioning, pleading voice.

But Dad looked quite miserable. Mum just kept on eating her egg and shrugged. 'Now don't make a fuss over nothing, Kit,' she said. 'Why don't you open that little present and see

what's inside. All of you – open your presents!'

There wasn't the usual happy feeling as the tissue paper came off, but, of course, they all loved their gifts. Daniel had a clever little penknife, disguised as a piece of bamboo; Kitty had a tiny box with a painted lid and a key; and Dad had a lovely polished wooden egg which opened to show some smart wooden cufflinks, nestling inside.

Daniel was looking cross. 'Dad, I can't believe you forgot to get something for Mum,' he said.

'It was all the rush to get away, and I'd been so busy at work,' said Dad unhappily.

'Well, *Mum* had a lot to do, and *Mum* was busy at work, and yet *Mum* remembered,' said Kitty, giving him her blackest look.

It was terrible. Mum ate her breakfast calmly, but Kitty knew she was a bit sad and hurt. Dad looked guilty. Daniel had that look on his face which says, 'I wish I could put this right but I don't know how to.' And that was just how Kitty felt, too.

So what could she do . . . ?

Then she thought of something – and it was like the sun coming out inside her head. As Dad rose to do the washing up, she took Dan aside and whispered to him. A few minutes later he asked Mum to come on a walk with him – a special long walk to a little hill that she loved. Since Dan was rather lazy and *never* suggested such things, she said yes right away.

So off they went. Kitty turned to Dad. 'Now!' she said, 'we've got work to do.'

Two hours later Mum and Dan came back, to find Dad and Kitty in the little cosy sitting room, looking pleased with themselves. The room was full of flowers and leaves, and in the middle of the coffee table was an Easter cake (a bit flat, but that didn't matter) decorated with primroses.

'Dad made it for you!' shouted Kitty.

'*Did* you?' asked Mum, smiling at him. He just nodded.

'Now look inside the yellow parcel!' Kitty was almost shouting – she was so excited.

Mum unfolded the yellow tissue paper (saved from the presents that morning) to reveal – a cardboard egg carton, painted lemon and green in a delicate, watery way. Her name was written in sky-blue on one of the sticky-out bits.

When she opened the carton, she gasped – because the ordinary thing had been made into a . . . 'work of art!', she said. Kitty had helped Dad find a lovely thing to go in each one of the six egg divisions. These are what they were: an empty snail shell, a very pretty stone, a small

white feather, a leaf, a curious piece of wood, and a little dried rose bud, found on a bush in the corner of the garden. It looked lovely.

'All things from *here* – so I'll always remember it,' said Mum happily.

'Happy Easter, love,' said Dad.

And – thanks to Kitty – it was.

I Know She's Awful . . .

Kitty told Daniel it would spoil her *whole* summer.

'Don't exaggerate,' sighed Mum.

'But it will – I know it will,' moaned Kitty.

Her cousin Melissa was coming to stay for a whole week, while Uncle Joe and Auntie Susan went away on their own.

'Ooh good, Kit,' giggled Daniel, 'you can play girly-wirly games together!'

'Very funny,' snapped Kitty.

She really didn't like Melissa – who liked her hair to be in ribbons and curls, and wore frilly dresses and couldn't bear to get dirty. Since Kitty was happiest in old jeans and boots, with her hair tangled and her hands in the soil . . . well, it really wasn't very good at all. And for a WHOLE WEEK!

Melissa arrived with a huge suitcase, which Dad carried up to Kitty's room. He put it down on Kitty's bed and said, 'You'll sleep here, Melissa.'

'But what about me?' gasped Kitty.

'We'll bring in the fold-up bed for you, Kit-kat, but people always give up their beds for guests.'

'Oh, do they?' said Kitty, grimly.

When they were alone, Melissa threw open the case, and asked Kitty to help her unpack. Piles of nice little frocks and skirts tumbled out on to the bed, as Melissa peered into Kitty's wardrobe with a snooty look on her face.

'Oh, there's not much room, is there?' she said. 'At home I've got a double wardrobe *and* a vanitory unit with a big mirror with bulbs round it, and a . . .'

But Kitty wasn't listening any more. 'A whole week of this!' she groaned to herself.

The days passed – and it was just as Kitty feared. Every time she suggested a game to play, Melissa complained that it was 'too rough', or 'too dirty', and suggested they set up a dolls' tea party. So Kitty's old bear, Mr Tubs, and her other bears and animals found themselves sitting with Melissa's three best dolls – and Kitty thought they didn't like it any more than she did!

But there was one thing that annoyed Kitty more than anything else. Melissa *knew* everything. Every time Kitty, or Mum, or Dad, or Daniel tried to tell her something, she tossed her curls and said, 'I know' – in a voice that drove Kitty mad.

Dad grinned when she whispered this to him. He said, 'The trouble is, she beats you at your own game!'

So by the end of the week Kitty was in a

really bad mood. William didn't like Melissa so he didn't come round, and Mum wouldn't let any of Kitty's schoolfriends visit because she said, 'Three is a bad number'. Melissa spoilt everything.

Now Saturday was the day of William's party. This year, for the first time, he was having a 'boys only' party, but said Kitty could come, because she was just like a boy.

Mum said Kitty had to take Melissa, and Kitty said it was impossible, so Mum said it wasn't fair for Kitty to go without Melissa, and then Melissa stuck her nose in the air and said she didn't want to play with stupid *boys* anyway . . .

When it got near the time William's friends and cousins were due to arrive, Kitty was so fed up she lost her temper, at last. 'Melissa, I think you're the most boring person I've ever met,' she shouted. 'Now, I'm going to my room and I just want a bit of peace, OK?'

'Well, if you feel like *that*,' said Melissa, and flounced off.

Kitty went upstairs and started to draw, and for a while she forgot her cousin. But after about an hour she thought she heard a strange noise coming from the wild hedge at the bottom of their garden. Or was it from next door? Maybe it was William's party. He had said they were just going to play outside until they were called in for tea . . .

Outside the kitchen door she stopped and listened. There were boys' voices, laughing – but wasn't that Melissa's voice too? Puzzled, she wandered down the garden, following the sound.

At the bottom of the garden, where the old fence met the wild hedge, the noise was really loud. There was laughter, and teasing, and in the middle of it all Melissa's voice saying, a bit tearfully, 'Just leave me alone'.

Kitty peered through one of the gaps in the fence – and there was Melissa, surrounded by boys who were making fun of her, imitating her voice and even pulling at her dress a little. William was there too, looking a bit uncomfortable. Melissa looked hot and unhappy.

Kitty didn't even stop to think. She just pushed her way through the rickety fence, and rushed to stand next to Melissa – glaring at the boys.

'What do you think you're doing?' she shouted.

'Just playing with Miss Melissa,' said one of William's big cousins in a high silly voice.

'Well, why don't you try to play with *me*?' asked Kitty, looking very fierce.

'Oh, Kit, it was only a bit of fun,' said William.

'Not much fun for Melissa,' said Kitty.

Melissa said nothing. She just stared at Kitty, sniffing quietly.

'But she's *awful*!' said William and one or two of the other boys, all together.

Kitty took a deep breath. 'I KNOW she's awful,' she said sternly, 'but she's *my cousin*! OK?'

The boys nodded, and moved away quietly. Kitty took Melissa firmly by the arm and pushed her through the hole in the fence. Her dress caught and tore, but Melissa didn't seem to notice. Then she told Kitty she'd wandered through to the next door garden and said silly things to the boys.

'So it was your fault really,' said Kitty.

'I know,' whispered Melissa.

'But they shouldn't have tried to bully you. Now listen to me, Melissa, there's a lot of things you don't know about games and boys and . . . and . . . everything. But if you listen to *me* I can tell you, and you'll have a lot more fun.'

Then Melissa did something astonishing. She just sat down in the dirt (not minding about her clothes) and looked up at Kitty.

'I know that, Kit,' she said, 'so will you start now?'

I Know I'm Right!

It was impossible, thought Kitty, to get through to Grown-ups. The G-U-s (as she had started to call them) always thought they were right. Or rather, they always KNEW they were right. It wasn't fair.

One day made her think this more than ever. It started in school, when Mrs Smith told the class that she *knew* that one of them must have broken the vase that she always had standing on her desk. She was very cross, and asked the guilty person to put up his or her hand.

No one did. All the children looked at each other, but nobody put up a hand. Then Mrs Smith went rather red. 'I know I'm right,' she said. 'It must be someone from this class. So if no one owns up I'll have to punish all of you.'

Then she told them she wouldn't take them on the outing she had planned; instead they

would have to stay in and learn some spellings.

'How does she *know* she's right?' Rosie asked Kitty at break. Kitty shrugged.

Dad collected Kitty from school as Mum had to go somewhere for her work – and usually it was a treat to walk home with Dad, because he was more likely to buy ice creams!

But tonight he was rather quiet – Kitty didn't know why.

'Are you cross, Dad?' she asked.

'Never mind,' he replied. (That was another thing which annoyed Kitty about the G-U-s. They always said, 'We'll see', or 'Never mind', instead of answering your questions.)

Mum came home soon after they got in, and Kitty found out that whatever made Dad grumpy was making Mum grumpy too. As she sat and watched television she heard them talking in the kitchen. Or rather, arguing.

'Oh no,' she thought, 'this is all I need!'

She crept out and listened. 'The trouble with you,' Dad said to Mum, 'is that you always think you're right.'

'So do you,' she replied.

'I do not,' he said.

'Yes, you do,' she said, in her 'that's-the-last-word' voice.

'There,' he said triumphantly, 'you always *know* you're right!'

'Gosh,' thought Kitty, 'they're worse than me and my friends! Honestly . . . G-U-s!'

She thought and thought, wondering what to do. First she had to find out what Mum and Dad were arguing about. So she went upstairs to see Dan, who was doing his homework.

'Oh yes,' he said, peering at his books, 'it

started this morning after Rosie's mum picked you up, and just before they both went to work. Mum said Dad had a bit too much to drink on their wedding day, and behaved badly, and he said he didn't.'

'Go on,' said Kitty.

'That's all,' shrugged Daniel.

'I don't believe it,' Kitty said, 'it's such a tiny thing.'

'Yes,' said Daniel, 'but they're both sure they're right!'

Kitty went downstairs, deep in thought. Then she went into the sitting room and phoned Gran.

'I know it's a funny thing to ask, Gran,' she said, 'but do you remember the day Mum and Dad got married?'

'Ooh, yes, of course!' said Gran, 'it was a lovely day . . .'

'Well, did Dad have a bit too much to drink?'

Gran started to giggle helplessly. 'Oh, it was so funny,' she said. 'He had lots of glasses of champagne, so that when he got up to make his speech, instead of just being boring and thanking everyone, he said he was the luckiest man in the world to be marrying such a beautiful, wonderful girl. And your mum blushed – especially when he gave her a big sloppy kiss in front of everyone. Then he fell over!'

'Thanks, Gran,' said Kitty, laughing.

She went into the kitchen, folded her arms and looked at them. 'A little bird called Gran just told me you had a bit too much to drink on your wedding day, Dad,' she said.

'There, I told you!' said Mum.

'But you didn't behave *badly*,' she went on.

'There!' said Dad.

'You see, you're both wrong *and* you're both right,' Kitty said, and told them just what Gran remembered.

Mum's face went all soft. 'Oh, you were *so* soppy,' she said.

'Yes, but it was a bit bad when my legs gave way!' said Dad, and they both started to laugh. And laugh, and laugh.

Kitty crept away – really pleased with

herself. And they had a happy family tea, with Mum and Dad telling lots of stories about the past, which Daniel and Kitty loved.

The next morning, when the class sat down for lessons, Mrs Smith stood up and coughed. 'Um, I've got something to say . . . One of the younger children owned up to rushing in here for some reason and knocking over my vase. So I was wrong to say it must have been one of you. I suppose we all make mistakes! And of course, we'll still go on our class outing.'

All the children cheered. But Kitty just thought, 'I don't know . . . G-U-s!'

I Know You Know!

Kitty felt sad – and very bad. She didn't quite understand why, but Daniel seemed to be getting all the attention. First, he had flu, so Mum and Dad took him lots of lovely meals in bed and made a great fuss of him.

Then he had his birthday, and there was a mountain of presents. Kitty felt very jealous. She knew she always had lots of presents for *her* birthday, but that was months and months away, and anyway, it didn't stop her feeling left out.

One week after that he had to take a special sort of exam, and so Mum and Dad made a great fuss again – helping him with his spellings, and his sums, and generally behaving as if there was nobody else in the world but Daniel.

Anyway, that was what Kitty thought.

She was in a great sulk, and started to be

very naughty, in lots of little ways.

Then one day Mum said, 'You must make sure the hamster is out of sight when Mrs Briggs comes for coffee.'

'Don't want to,' mumbled Kitty crossly.

And when posh Mrs Briggs was talking to Mum in the sitting room, she very quietly opened the door and let Sandy walk across the carpet, just by her feet.

'Aaaaagh,' screamed Mrs Briggs, spilling her coffee all over her suit and the chair. 'It's a mouse! Eeeeeek!'

'No, it's not, it's my pet hamster,' said Kitty, running in to grab Sandy.

After that, she was in big trouble. They had planned a family outing to the cinema, but Mum said Kitty couldn't go.

'Why not?' asked Kitty.

'Because you've been naughty.'

'But you promised!' wailed Kitty.

'Yes, but you were very mean to frighten poor old Mrs Briggs,' said Mum.

'It's not fair,' shouted Kitty.

Then Dad came in, and Mum told him what had happened, and they agreed that Dad would take Daniel to the cinema on his own. Kitty sat on the top stair and sulked.

When Daniel came home from school (late, because he'd been to a club) Kitty heard him tell Mum and Dad he'd had a bad day because he had forgotten his glasses.

'Silly thing,' said Mum, gently.

'*If that was me they'd shout*,' muttered Kitty to herself. Now she felt *really* sad and bad.

She looked into Daniel's room, saw his glasses case on his table, and a wicked idea came into her mind. She slipped in, picked it up, and went into her own room. Then, looking innocent, she walked downstairs.

After tea, Dad frowned at Kitty and said it was time to take Daniel to the cinema. 'Go upstairs and get your specs, Dan,' he added.

Kitty sat very still as Daniel went upstairs, wanting to hug herself with glee when he yelled, 'I can't find them!'

'Look properly,' Mum called.

'I *have*,' he shouted. 'I know I left my glasses case on my desk, and now I can't find it.'

Dad ran up to help, and there was a lot of noise as feet ran to and fro. At last Daniel and Dad came down, shaking their heads, and Mum dashed up to his bedroom to look. All the time Kitty just sat there, looking innocent.

Mum came down at last, looking very puzzled. Dad looked at his watch. 'Well, it's getting late,' he said, 'but if we don't find them there's no point in going. It'll hurt your eyes too much.' Daniel nodded sadly.

When Kitty heard that she was glad. Her plan had worked. And she felt so wicked that, in her mind, she saw herself with two little horns and a pointed tail! *That'll serve them right for being mean to me*, she thought.

There must have been a glint in her eye, because suddenly Daniel looked closely at her.

'Do you know where they are, Kitty?' he asked.

'What, me? No – why?' said Kitty.

Something in her voice made Mum and Dad look at her too.

'Where are they, Kit?' asked Dad.

'How should I know?' Kitty replied.

At that, Mum frowned. 'I know you know,' she said.

'How do you know I know?' asked Kitty.

'Because I do,' said Mum.

'Well, I don't. So there!' said Kitty, folding her arms.

'She *does* know! I know she knows,' cried Daniel.

'Well, if you know so much, why don't you go and get them then!' said Kitty.

Dad groaned. 'This isn't getting us anywhere,' he said. 'And I was really looking forward to our family outing tonight.'

'Kitty spoilt it,' said Daniel.

Then Kitty stopped feeling bad and just felt sad. Very sad. So sad she wanted to cry. 'It's not my fault,' she mumbled, getting very red in the face.

Mum saw she was upset, and sat down next to her. 'Whose fault is it?' she asked.

'Yours.'

'Why?'

Then everything Kitty had been feeling for the last few weeks came out in a great big blurt. They all listened quietly.

'So that was why you were being extra naughty?' asked Mum.

'Yes,' Kitty sniffled, 'because I thought you loved Daniel better than me.'

'Silly thing,' said Dad gently, 'as if that could be true! We love you *both* – and I think you know that, don't you Kit?'

'I *know* she knows,' smiled Mum.

Kitty smiled, and nodded her head.

'Well, if we rush we'll just make it,' said Dad, 'but first, we'd better find those specs.'

Kitty beckoned them to follow her, then threw open the cupboard in her bedroom. And there was Mr Tubs sitting on the shelf, with Daniel's glasses perched on his nose!

They laughed and laughed. 'Oh, Kit,' spluttered Dan, 'he looks just like our headmaster.'

'No, he doesn't,' laughed Dad, 'I know who he looks like . . . He looks like . . .'

And Mum screamed, 'Mrs Briggs!'